The Killing Fields and Other Poems

NAHSHON COOK

The Killing Fields and Other Poems

ISBN: 978-0-9907958-1-0

Library of Congress Control Number: 2014950655

Published by Shabda Press
Pasadena, CA 91107
www.shabdapress.com

Acknowledgments

The Elephant and the Mahout– Loch Raven Review
Something My Mom Told Me This Morning on the Phone– Splinter Generation
Last Night– Splinter Generation
The Killing Fields 1, 2, 3 & 4– Euonia Review
Loneliness:1– Commonline Journal
The Leper– Dm Du Jour
Penpals:1– L'Allure des Mots
Today– L'Allure des Mots
Love– L'Allure des Mots
For People Confusing Young Black Men, Like Myself, With Deer During Hunting Season– L'Allure des Mots
Everyday People:3– L'Allure des Mots
From a Conversation-Hour Discussion About Intolerance with Adult English Students– Split This Rock
Moo Moo– Yes, Poetry
Erawan Museum– Rose and Thorn
The Classical Khon Dancer– Rose and Thorn
The Flood:1– Rose and Thorn
Words– Origami Poetry Project
Nonthaburi Immigration– Origami Poetry Project
Last Night,– Killer Tree Ink, Epic Rites Press

For My Mommy

Table of Contents

The Beginning

The future
is bleak,

uncertain
and beautiful:

this is the thought
I arrived at

this morning
after being awakened

by the sound
of angel wings

flapping
in my living room.

Something My Mother Told Me This Morning on the Phone

If you don't see the light, don't stay.

Today

today I saw
a man in the market

wearing a t-shirt
that said

we lose and learn
so that we can live

which left me
with the thought

of how nice it would be
to keep dreaming

of China
but how once I go there

I won't be able
to dream anymore
—

There's something unutterably
painful and liberating

about walking the earth
in full knowledge

that you're going to die
that you won't be around forever

3

and about being reminded that
that's what life's about isn't it

having
by letting go

Nepal Poems
Reworked #1: A Leper

She sits on the side of the street
atop a bundle of rags
with a copper begging bowl in front of her
and a naked, brown, chubby-cheeked baby boy
cradled in the handless stump of an arm
at her right breast suckling milk
while she pleads for grace
from the crowded stream of passers-by
with her other bloody, swaddled nub
and a pus-filled, sore-splotched face
lacking eyebrows and the two fleshy parts
where lips should be

The Erawan Museum

this hand crafted
three-headed

bronze elephant
has a spiraling

wooden staircase
built inside

the mural painted hollow
of its right hind leg

that transplants you
up into the sculpture's belly

where there's a relic
of Lord Buddha

housed in the crown
of a golden idol

which is just one
among many

beautiful
long ago things

whose makers
are not named

The Killing Fields (1): The Stupa

when you reach
the front gate of the Killing Fields
you're welcomed
by a magnificently stunning
chalk-white reason for the living
to forever hold dear
the corpselike memory
of the dead
whose sealed glass encased
blow-bearing skulls
are stacked
tier upon tier upon tier
like file cabinet drawers
in this large concrete
memorial stupa's
tall rectangular
four-sided shape
hatted in a roof
with four gold-trimmed gables
and a white spire
that shoots up from the center
like a majestic snow-capped mountain peak
pointing its pyramidal finger
up to the cloudless soft blue-if-it's-a-boy-blue sky
as if attempting
to stay in sweet melodious tune
with heaven
like the balletic streams of grey smoke

wafting up from a potted bouquet
of red-stemmed incense
burning as Buddhist funeral rites
at the hallowed feet
of this lordly shrine

The Killing Fields (2): The Baby-Killing Tree

then there was the baby-killing tree
beside the mass grave for women and infants
where the little ones were hung upside down
and their heads swung back and forth
like the pendulum-bob of a grandfather clock
into this huge tree's solid bloodstained trunk
until their little baby brains were beaten to a pulp
like the soft fleshy part of a grapefruit
while their mothers helplessly watched
as the short lived lives of children
they'd ushered into this world
were snatched away from the tight grip of their maternal love
like carrots from the earth

The Killing Fields (3):
The Mass Graves

And I saw bits of sun-bleached bone and teeth
along with the surviving threadbare shreds of clothing
from some of the people whose bodies were tossed
into these, now hallowed, craters
after having been executed
like ceremonial rites in a religious sacrifice
as I walked along the little serenely slithering path
from and to each painted white wooden sign
with bold-lettered black writing that marked the largest graves
with an account of the cold-blooded hard-heartedness that had been unearthed;
while at the same time letting the barefaced, joy-filled laughter
of little children playing in the courtyard of the school next door
caress my ears like a loving touch
as I read: *"mass grave of more than 100 victims,
children and women, whose majority were naked",*
"mass grave of 166 victims without heads",
"mass grave of 450 victims", etc. etc. etc.

The Killing Fields (4):
A Prayer

By the end of my walk of remembrance
I wanted to pray,
and needed to pray,
and even tried to pray.
But still, I was unable to. Amen.

A Classical Khon Dancer

crowned in a gold pagoda

she very slowly makes her way around the stage

with impossibly shaped, wheeling hands

arced back into elegant crescent-fingered fans

while her carefully mastered incarnation

gently sways from side-to-side

in a deeply-felt, flowing dance

atop angled legs and flexed feet so silkily placed

she appears to be floating

on the unearthly xylophone-and-wooden flute song

played by a small band of live musicians

Pron

I was standing on the bank
of the Mekong River,

watching the sunset,
when an old man in a blue beanie

came up and asked my name,
where I was from, my age,

and if I was married;
then spelled out, letter for letter,

that his name was Pron,
and that he was born in Thailand,

that he was sixty-two,
and that he had two sons

who were thirty and thirty-one,
and that he worked as an angler.

I asked if there were still any of those huge
350 kilo catfish in the river.

Pron shook his head *No*
and positioned his arms

as if he were holding a shotgun,
whose trigger he pulled

with the index finger of his right hand
and said: *Pow! Too many people fishing.*

Self-Portrait As Tameca

Sometimes, I wake up
in this same apartment
and don't even know where I am.
Things are familiar
and at the same time
unfamiliar. I come home
and am so grateful
knowing that this place is my place,
but really feeling outside of it somehow,
like I am learning about
the person who lives here,
waiting for her to come home.

Penpals: 8

Last night, I tried, again, to re-work a poem I would've thrown out years ago, were it not for the last six words reminding me that I'm still inside of a human body exploring time and what has to die before I force myself to change.

In the poem, there's small figurine of the Virgin Mary gracefully draped in a white gown flowing down around her feet, on a coffee table, across from a grandfather clock in someone's living room–I'm not sure whose. A long, blue veil covers everything on her slightly tilted and lowered head except the glassy face.

I've tried to find a way to talk about her hands–how the left one is raised in a permanent blessing, while the right holds a gold roasry–but, haven't had much luck in including those details.

The church I grew up in, as a little boy, had an effigy of Jesus hanging scarecrow-armed on a giant wooden cross on the wall behind the pulpit. His thorn-crowned head dangling–delicately–from his shoulders like a fly in an abandoned cobweb.

I have this thing that really freaks me out about not realizing I've begun writing the wrong life story until I reach its end: I don't fear dying, I fear not having lived first. I fear the regret of not having taken a few deep breaths and letting the perfection of this earth, as it is, give itself to me. I fear not feeling the joys of loving without fear. I fear not being able to pray. I fear living lost. I fear not loving well enough. I fear not having anything to be thankful for. I fear being angry at the best I could have been, had I tried when I had a chance.

It rained all day today. In fact, the clouds are still crying. I want to live between their tears.

Alex: 1

1)
This evening, while soaking in a tub, I found myself in the memory of me and Alex's first date at Fuji. We were seated at a circular Teakwood table right next to a huge window, the other side of which two little fat boys sumo wrestled outside on a huge grey flagstone that doubled as their ring. They crouched down, each with their hands on their knees, slammed their right leg on the ground and then their left before waddling towards each other with outstretched hands and collided in a big belly bump. The little fat boy with the brown Band-Aid on his chin, lost.

2)
Back at my apartment, we sat on my couch, sipped tea and talked some more. During the course of our conversation, Alex asked me to tell him something true. So I did. Then he told me about the time he caught his ex-boyfriend in their bed with another man. And that the reason he hadn't left sooner was because he felt like the only other alternative for him at that particular stage in his life was going back into the world of being a single gay man trying to reassure himself he won't die a bitter old lonely queen. *"But, what, really, is the purpose of our lives,"* he mused, *"if not to face our fears as beautifully as we can—and grow?"*

China Poem:
On The Way Home

I saw a lady die today.
She was crossing the street

when a blue-and-white taxi
came vrooming down the road.

Her head shattered
the car's windshield.

The medics arrived
and covered

everything but her feet
with a hospital-white sheet,

then lit a cigarette
and watched

the police officer write
the taxi driver a ticket.

After they'd finished their smokes
the two men loaded the lady's body

into the ambulance
and drove away.

When I got home and
told my roommate this story,

He said: *Well,*
shit happens.

China Poem:
Carefour Supermarket

I was standing
in one of the checkout lines

when a middle-
aged woman

started screaming
at an old man,

accusing him
of stealing

cuts of meat
from a grocery basket

parked on the other side
of the rail

where she stood
cursing and

making grabs
for the plastic bag

full of claims
from the kill,

which the old man
clucthed to his chest

like hunger
was the only thing

he trusted enough
to believe in.

China Poem: Breakfast

This morning,
at breakfast,

I recieved
another affirmation

that there are no
perfect relationships:

I was chewing
a piece of toast

when my teeth
bit my tongue.

And they're in
the same head.

China Poem: A Baby Girl

The leaves
were glazed in frost

this morning
when a baby girl

was found dead
on the sidewalk

next to the green recycle bin
at the bus stop,

opposite the market,
not too far from my flat.

On the evening news
they showed ambulance staff

watching an old trash picker
in a black rabbit fur hat

bag the baby's body
in a white burlap sack

that he tied down tight
to the rack

on the back of his scooter
then drove away.

Penpals: 2

I've never had a girlfriend. Once, when I was in high school, one of my girl cousin's best friends had a crush on me. One evening they came over to the house. The friend brought a red rose and asked me to be her prom date. That was one of the scariest moments of my life.

I told her I'd let her know tomorrow at school. I didn't. I never spoke to her again. That night I had a dream about trying to be normal, and going to the dance with this girl:

All I could see was the both of us in a hotel room, after prom, and me not being able to make our situation work. And how she might imagine that my limper was her fault. When in-fact, I think, it was just being made clear to me that girls were never going to be my cup of tea.

—

My mom flies home tomorrow. At one point, during our conversation over breakfast this morning, she said: Well, once you stop running after what you think will make you happy and stop running from what you think will make you sad, you find yourself. And that's a good place to be.

—

Also, this afternoon, on our way back from the rose gardens in Nakhom Pathom, we saw an elephant jaywalk across to the other side of the highway, where it plodded in the emergency lane against on-coming traffic. When it began to rain again, the elephant's mahout laid his bull-hook across the top of the elephant's head and opened a bright-pink umbrella.

I tried to get a good picture of the pair as we drove past but the shot came out blurry.

—

This evening, on our way to the skytrain from dinner, we saw a woman sitting on a step under a streetlight looking sad and like she'd been awake too many hours with no sleep.

Her hair was pulled back in a few-days-old ponytail. A boy, of about twelve, was draped across her lap, wrapped in a stained pink blanket with closed eyes and mouth agape.

The back of his head was cradled in her left arm her right hand palmed a moist white cloth against his feverish, glowing brow. He looked very sick, and like, maybe, he was dying.

There was no plastic cup for handouts at the woman's feet.

A Prayer In Bangkok

I was just strolling
when I glanced
into a shrubbery space
on the side of the sidewalk
and saw a single
white lotus blossom
balanced high
in the air
atop a perfectly postured
hollow green stem
rooted beneath
the sooty pond's
polished black surface

For People Confusing Young Black Men, Like Myself, with Deer During Hunting Season: Written in Response to George Zimmerman's Exoneration By the Florida State Court

1)

Last night, I sat in my room like a Mongolian lark looking out the window from behind the bars of its bamboo cage at a sparrow in the tree,—and feeling like a flower pot that never leaves the front porch, while I prayed to Erato for a story that would make me human again. She arrived dressed in a pair of big, carrot-orange butterfly wings outlined in white, polka-dotted black trim. After I'd grabbed something to write with, she recited this poem for me:

2)

I see you, She said, there, trying to look away from the convicting eyes of that nigger dangling from Lady Liberty's right wrist. The whip that jolted the buckboard forward and caused that nigger's neck to snap like a twig was the lion's roar. In India they say: *Sometimes the lion must roar to remind the horse of its fear.* You won't be able to stop looking at that nigger until that nigger's body stops swaying in the breeze. Life is worth more than a price. That nigger is you.

3)
Stop running from your demons, She said. Demons are the shit from which angels bloom and heal the refugeed undead exiled in your heart—with love's true aloe, like a shaman. Goodbye.

Love

This morning
I found myself

cocooned in the limbs
of a man

sleeping next to me
who last night

(while I made my way
down to his cock)

wanted to know
if I was in love with him

I paused and asked
what he meant by love

he said

that space
between us

where we
leave ourselves

and meet
each other

From A Conversation-Hour Discussion about Intolerance with Adult English Students: 1

Then he explained
how the Buddha

instructed us
to reflect on the body

our skin
our hands and feet

our body hair
our nails and teeth

our noses
our eyes

our minds
our hearts

so that we can see
ourselves clearly

in every person
no matter where

A Run Away Slave

Said she was fourteen
    and that the man she worked for
    abused her
Said he kicked her everytime she didn't learn
    how he liked his house cleaned
    so she could be his maid
Said he threatened to sell her into prostitution
    and paid her in food and board
Said she walked to Thailand from Laos
    after escaping from her father
    because her best friend told her
    she could make a lot of money
Said she walked through the jungle alone
    and drank dirty stream water
Said she needed help returning home
She didn't seem afraid.
She liked chocolate and almond covered
    Magnum ice cream bars.

The Flood

1.
An elephant
with pink-speckled skin

around the edges of its ears
and on its trunk

is being ridden past
a submerged quarter-ton pick-up truck

on a flooded street
in Ayutthaya.

The article below the photograph
goes on to talk about

how the modern day mammoth
and her master

have been helping to rescue
stranded people.

2.
I watched a woman walk across the street
while I looked down from my bedroom window

wondering what our village would look like
under all of the water they say is coming.

From Another Conversation with One of My Seven Year Old Students: 2

Him: While I was vacation in Hua Hin,
    I heard that a guy went into the cinema
    and killed fourteen people who were watching Batman.
    My daddy said he was dressed like the Joker.

Me: What do you think about that?

Him: I think he's going to Hell when he dies.

Me: What's Hell like?

Him: It's down. Opposite of the heavens. It's a mean place.
    When he's there, monsters will eat him
    and he won't be reborn as a person ever again.

Me: So have you gone to see Batman?

Him: No. Somebody told my daddy and my daddy told me
    that the movie wasn't fun.
    Besides, I'm scared of going to the cinema
    and getting shot like those people did.

Penpals: 1

1)
Every night, at about this time, it rains. It's raining now. The sound of raindrops parachuting from the sky like a stampeding herd of fallen angels, and hitting the tops of things down below, reminds me of belly-aching, joyous laughter. But when I look at the window pane, and watch the clear little droplets drip, ever so slowly, I think unhappy tears.

Sometimes, I wish I wasn't who I was. But I am. Earlier this evening, at dinner, I talked to my heart about this and asked her why. She said, "My dear, your life is an unfinished puzzle whose pieces are still being put in their place." I think it's the sick, weakened slivers of ourselves that make us beautiful. It's in the rubble, after a hurricane, that the survivor's strength is found.

And I understand the cut off foreigner feeling, very well. I think it seems to stick with people who miss home and are ready to go back, but aren't really sure if they want to. There are many crowds of people here that I don't fit into. Sometimes, it feels like finding someone to have meaningful conversation with is close to impossible because so many folks seem to think thinking is a sin. I'm grateful for books. Love.

In my way of seeing, there is no love without understanding. There's no me without you, or anyone else. This place is a sad place. But, it's also an alive and beautiful place that will grow you to the point of blossoming, if you let it. Or, it will swallow you up whole and make you forget you ever even tried to exist. The magic thing about it, like everything else in life, is in the ability to choose who we are, and will be, honestly. It's terribly scary. But, it's all there is. Love.

But, what is love? I want to know. That's why I dropped out of seminary: the professor's minds were overflowing with felled forests. Their hearts, desert sands praying for rain with words that left my insides feeling cold and rigamortis. Since then, I've traveled and been to many places. And have learned that places are places because people are in them. And that people are beautiful, but that beautiful is only good when we stay alive to the fact that all of our hearts are stained by hurt, and we help each other scrub them clean with wire sponges and scouring cleanser. I am a pilgrim journeying. This is as far as I've gotten. Love.

2)

The comforts of language are true and deep, right? And, I'm by no means a perfectionist. I'm just trying to figure out who I am. I believe in the process of things, especially human beings and flowers. That's why I write: because if I I didn't, I feel like I'd disappear. And I sometimes do. Then, I usually find myself (on my off day) in the back of a cab, on my way to the bookstore wondering what it'd be like to be a butterfly, or some other something.

3)

I'm a silly man. Sometimes, maybe even foolish. But, I trust myself. And that has never failed me. And even though it sometimes feels like I'm living in five-hundred years ago, life keeps teaching me that I can either learn what I need to learn, or run away and be a second-hand human being. And since I've begun to forget how to be afraid, I've been seeing love as intuition as opposed to forgiveness. Which has opened my heart to a deeper way of being in the world, feelingly, and trusting that space where I can let go of the pain with all my might. There's nothing left to forgive. Love has no opposite. That's where the value of art is for me. It helps me understand the nature of my hurt, so that I can heal.

4)

Poetry is the angel of love and memory. I'm her acolyte. To study her is to attempt understanding the alien universe that is another person and finding yourself instead. Currently, I'm learning how to look back and stop wishing the past were different. When I came out to my parents, I wrote them each a poem. That was a good thing. It put the son they had to death so the son they have could live.

Live right now, live forever.

5)

A choir of toads is croaking like crows. Their songs are comforting. Some of them will be pancaked on the cement by people driving off to work in the morning. Art favors the risk takers, right? It's stopped raining. The streetlamps have found their reflection in water puddles. Light.

Peace and smile,

Nahshon

Last Night,

I watched my fear of life
tie one end of a long piece

of twine around its neck
and the other end to a roof beam

before it sat down
and went to sleep forever

A Working Girl

The truck parked
a few feet

in front of her,
so she walked up

to the driver's
side window.

The two talked
for a little while

before the truck
pulled away,

slowly, as if
the driver

were giving her
one last chance

to change her mind
and accept his offer.

But instead
she returned

to her space
on the sidewalk

right next to the curb,
not too far

from where I stood
watching while I waited

for a taxi driver who'd stop
so I could get home.

A China Poem: Lunch Conversation with A Local: 1

1)

Him: Are you on Jesus' team?
Me: What do you mean?
Him: Do you believe in Jesus?
Me: I study his teachings, yes.
Him: Do you go to church?
Me: No, not often.
Him: I don't believe in anything.
Me: Are you okay with that?
Him: Not Jesus, not Buddha... No need.
Me: You're lucky.
Him: No, it doesn't make sense.
Me: Ok.
Him: Why do you read Jesus' book?
Me: It helps my heart love better.
Him: You're a mutant.
Me: Maybe. I don't know.
Him: We're the same person.
Me: Yes.

2)

Him: You know Tibet?
Me: Yes, I'd like to go there.
Him: Hmm, no. Not yet.
　　　Tibet's not liberated
　　　like Hong Kong.
　　　But, almost. Soon.
Me: OK.

Him: China's like a father,
     Tibet's his lost son.
     The father went out,
     found his son
     and is bringing him back home.
Me: And what do you think about that?
Him: I have no idea.

Nepal Poems Reworked
#5: At Pashupatinath

I sat on one of the ancient temple's stone steps
directly across from the red-hot flames
on the other side of the holy river Bagmati
and watched people's corpses be reduced to dust
by the golden straw fed fires of funeral pyres
pouring out clouds of fog grey smoke into the sky

Nonthaburi Immigration

1)
Forty-five minutes into the taxi ride
to the immigration office
the driver realized he'd lost us.
So, he parked on the side of the road
and asked for help from a few different
passing pedestrians
which landed us at a Visa stamping office
for Thais wanting to go to Cambodia.

By now he was quite upset.
So, he hailed another taxi,
gave the driver the paper with the directions on it,
kicked me out of his car and drove off.

When we arrived
the taxi driver tried to charge me
eighty baht more than the meter said I owed.
I gave him exact change
and thanked him for his help.

2)
I was in line, reading my book,
waiting for my number to be called
when a monk from Cambodia
came up behind me, looked over my shoulder
and asked what I was reading.

He was musky, so I smelled him
before I turned around and saw him.
When I did, he was smiling a smile
full of plaque enameled teeth
that looked like they'd gone to bed
and woken up the next morning
without being brushed for a few days.

During the course of our conversation
he shared that he was studying
for his Master's degree in comparative philosophy,
and that he sometimes gets migraines
from reading so much. When I suggested
he go to the eye doctor to see if he might need glasses,
he shook his head 'no' saying he uses the pain
as an invitation to practice and deepen his meditation.
Then he asked where I lived,
how much I paid for rent
and if he could have my phone number.

3)
The taxi ride back to my flat was pleasant:
the driver was lovely enough to offer me watermelon
after wrongly assuming I was a professional soccer player.
He even turned the radio down
while I talked with mom on the phone
and shared with her the story about the monk.
But, he also tried to charge me eighty baht
more than the meter said I owed.

Then She Told Me This Story

Rumor has it
he murders Myanmar people
and buries their bodies in his land.

He has one hundred horses
on a thousand acres
and it's hard for the help
to escape once they arrive.
His stable is way out in the country.

It's a very beautiful place
in the forest
and has wild peacocks walking around.

Once, we went for a visit
and saw servants
whose hands had been hacked off,

probably because they stole something.
Which I can understand, she said,
but I don't believe he's a killer.

China Poem: Last Night

Last night
I walked out the office
and saw a young woman
sitting on the sidewalk
in front of a bar.
The only thing keeping her
from faceplanting
was a man in a black T-shirt,
holding her right wrist.
He was yelling,
and was red-faced,
and looked more worried than angry.
He kept trying to call a taxi,
none would stop. Maybe
the drivers caught sight
of the spit-up clumps of food in her hair,
and were afraid
she would vomit
in the backseat
of their car.

It began to rain.
I opened my umbrella
and spent the rest of the walk home
thinking about
that place
deep inside of us
that's not trying
to do anything
except live.

A Beautiful Story

1)

A little tangled spring of tight, black, corkscrew shaped ringlets streams down in a trail of kinky curls past his navel, and to his crotch where they cling, like algae to a rock, in a thick pubic beard of spirally, coarse, threadlike strands of hair at the base of his erection;

around which the callused hoop of his right palm moves up and down until he relaxes his head back onto the pillow with closed eyes and comes all over his soft, brown belly.

2)

The next morning at breakfast he asked me to tell him a beautiful story:

Well, I said, when I first moved to Thailand I spent some time in Chaing Mai and became friends with a Buddhist monk with whom I shared a story about a famous Estonian artist who liked to paint in convents. And how one day she asked one of the nuns if she could paint her portrait. The nun told the painter, 'See that hog in the mud? Paint it and call it Sister Maria.'

The monk smiled and said: *'It's very important that people learn not to expect too much.'*

Moo-Moo

we were sitting
at one of the tables

at 2Bar
talking about

how bad a sign it was
that the ambulance

parked across the sidewalk
from the front door

wasn't in a hurry
to get back to the hospital

when we got word
from his older brother

that our friend
Moo-Moo

was found dead
about an hour earlier

upstairs
in his room

I hope Moo-Moo
didn't kill himself

R. said,
but I understand if he did

China Poem: Walking

I pass a scraggily dressed man
towing a six-foot-high load
of flattened cardboard boxes down the street
in a wooden, two-wheeled cart
with handle-ends tucked under his armpits
like shafts in the tugs of carriage horse's harness.

A few minutes later, a street sweeper pedals by
on tricycle with a square metal trash box
built in-between the two back wheels.
In the box is a bamboo handled broom
with bristles made of pruned twigs
fringed in crispy, olive-drab green leaves.

When I arrive at the corner
and wait for the signal to cross to turn green,
a black Porsche with black windows
pulls up behind the number 118 bus in the turning lane.

I stand there thinking about
my breakfast run to the supermarket
to buy oatmeal and yogurt and fruit
and seeing the plucked,
pimply carcasses of chickens
laid out on a big tin tray
with slit throats
and a thin little red spill
leaking from their beaks.

China Poem: Playground

I saw a little boy
fall down and cry

on my way
to work today.

His grandmother
looked back,

said, *Get up,*
and kept walking.

So, the little boy
quieted himself,

dried his tears,
and continued

running towards
the playground.

Everyday People: 3

Last night
three men

passed us
on the sidewalk

carrying
the limp body

of an unconcious woman
with big

saliva bubbles
bubbling up

from her mouth
like boiling water.

R. thought
her lungs were flooded

and that she
was going to die.

I don't know,
I said,

but those guys
either have really

good good hearts
or are about to do

something
awful.

A China Poem: Lunch Conversation with A Local: 2

Him: What is God?

Me: I don't know.
   But, I once asked
   one of my students
   this same question.

Him: And what did he say?

Me: That God is all over the place,
   and doesn't have a body,
   but lives in everyone's heart,
   and bones; like someone
   who owns a bunch of houses
   but has no home
   with babies and toilets
   and toys.

Him: How old was this boy?

Me: Four.

Him: Wow. What else
   did he say?

Me: That choices
   are magic things.

The Elephant and the Mahout

This evening
I was out to dinner with friends,
when a mahout
came riding down the street
on a young elephant
who, at the command of its handler,
let off little trumpet bursts from its trunk
in an attempt to scavenge some income
off of restaurant patrons with its cuteness.–
Which it did! And why not?
People got up from their dinner tables
with money in-hand, walked outside
and paid to touch and feed and take pictures
with this hairy headed,
thick-skinned baby giant
whose soft, deep-seeing brown eyes
were like a grace-given peek into the window
of how unfathomable a miracle life is.

A Christmas Poem

I am
a man,

fragile and full
of mistakes.

I do many things
I don't understand.

But, I think that's where
the hidden treasure is:

in the darkness
that must be there

so that light
can come.

Korn

I took ice and was in a five man orgy
that was recorded by a guy
who has the tape and isn't answering my calls.
Now, I'm worried that if the video gets out to people I know
they'll all think I'm a bad man.
Everytime I think about it...
I can't stop the tears. I've been crying for two days.
I want to be happy. I don't know why I did it.
I have money, a car and houses. I don't have a perfect body,
but I do have a nice shape. I don't know why no one loves me.
Every man I've ever loved has hurt me. I'm afraid of love.
I don't know why no one loves me.
Thai guys only want sex three or four times
and then they are finished.
The last boyfriend I had was a twenty-nine year old perfect body.
He gave me a key to his room.
So, one day I went there and caught him
having sex with another man... it hurt me so bad.
If I told my Thai friends what happened on Saturday
the whole country would know in two days.
If my parents found out,
it would be better for me to kill myself:
they don't know I'm gay.
In Thailand, if parents have a gay son
everyone will think
they did something wrong.
And I thought if I told you,
you wouldn't talk to me anymore.

"That's why you canceled dinner?"

"Yes," he said, "because I didn't want you to see my sadness."

Words

I was in bed thinking about
how we spend our whole life

preparing for the moment we're in
when I began wishing words

were able to give voice
to more than they are able to

and that there was enough time
for that expression to be heard

but I'm seeing that most things
come in stages

and that if I take them
as they come

and with attention
I can learn what they teach

and hopefully
move beyond their limits

before my long night's journey into day
comes to an end

From A Conversation with My Seven Year Old Student: 8

Him: I have a riddle for you?

Me: Ok?

Him: If you walk in a dark room
       and the light is only there
       because you are,
       what does that mean?

Me: I don't know?

Him: It's means, you are the light.

Alone

Dear God
>> since we've
>>>> been talking

more honestly
>> and openly and
>>>> often about things

I've realized
>> that I'm lonelier
>>>> with you here

Penpals: 7

I saw a brown and white kitten on my way home from work today. I knelt down to pet it till my knees hurt, then I went on my way, thinking about the conversation I had with my mom this morning. She told me this year marks her seventh in remission.

—

After I got off the phone with my mom, I took a shower. I stood feeling the water fall on my body like rain, when I remembered the nurse who helped with my mom's needle biopsy, and who told me the truth when I asked if there was a cure for cancer. *Hun*, she said, *if there were, the doctor wouldn't be able to give your mom his card.*

—

Instead of radiation, my mom chose to have both of her breasts removed.

The morning after she returned home from the hospital, the surgeon called explaining how the post-biopsy showed what the mammogram hadn't: the cancer had spread to her right breast.

—

Everything happening in the world has already happened. In life, only life. In death, only death.

Four Months Later

1)

It was rainy and grey this morning on the tarmac. But, when we lifted above the clouds, sunshine flooded the cabin. The woman next to me, in the window seat, pulled our shade down and went back to sleep. I, on the other hand, sat thinking about how time has changed. The day fades away much more slowly, now, and suddenly is gone. Then comes the night, where I curl-up like a fetus in the silence at the center of the dark and listen to myself listening for signs of light.

2)

There's a beautiful Chinese proverb that says: *Hard times make for good poetry.* And so, here I am, on a chair, in LAX, with my notebook and pen, trying to write towards an answer while I wait for my flight home so I can help my mom fight her second bout with cancer.

Driving to the Hospital

It rained this morning
on our way to the hospital.

The wiper blades
moved back-and-forth

leaving streaked arcs
across the windshield.

As we turned right at the light
onto Havana from Alameda,

she lowered the volume
on the radio and said:

We either go after it hard
or cancer kills me.

I can't afford to be afraid,
it's too expensive.

I agreed then asked
if she remembered

our phone converation
while I was in Thailand

when she told me:
"With everyday we're given,

we're given another chance
to change

the rest of our lives
forever."

No, she said, *I don't
remember saying that.*

*But, I'm glad
you're home.*

Mom in Prayer

My faith is strong
>with it, I can fight
>>till the end

I just don't understand
>why the end keeps trying
>>to come so soon

God, that's the part
>of our conversation
>>I just don't undestand

Am I sayin' the wrong thing

Am I asking the wrong question

Anyway,
>whatever the reason
>>I don't accept it

A Guy Talking on the Phone in the Radiology Waiting Room

My mind isn't as clear as it should be, but let me pull out my calender.

It's on the brain.

I'm here at the hospital, waiting to get an MRI.

Yes, I start chemo on the first.

And yes, It would be nice for you to be here.

But, that's impossible.

And why wish for the impossible?

I know you're not putting yourself in debt, but you've got the girls' college
    to worry about.

I have a chemo treatment the Monday of Columbus Day weekend.

If I'm up to it, I'll come out that Wednesday to Connecticut.

I can have my secretary book me a flight.

No problem.

Yes, I'm sure.

We'll all have a few nice days together.

It'll be good for me to be with you and the grandkids.

My Mom Speaking
to Her Surgeon

Too many
Black women

are dying
from breast cancer.

You know
the statistics.

No! We don't
have to debate anything.

I just want to know
what you would

tell your kids
if you were trying

to do everything
in your power

to be proactive
and your doctors

told you *"no"*
and there was nothing else

you could do
to try'n save yourself

aside from
keep asking for help?

How do you think
their lives would change

because they care
about you?

Angels

Mom and I were driving
past the cemetery

where my great-grandparents
and my grandma are buried.

And I was telling her
how I'd just seen

the second dove in a week
on my way to pick her up

When she said: *I have to
tell you what just happened:*

*I just saw them
waving at me.*

Who? Your mom
and Grandma and Grandpa?

Yes. she said, *And my dad
and Uncle Charles.*

*They were all smiling
and waving.*

*And it was just
their faces and hands.*

You're gonna
be okay! I said.

I already am okay, she said,
the angels've got me.

Penpals: 10

1)
Once, I went to Siam Paragon to buy some books at the bookstore, which is on the third floor. On my way up, there was a line of people on the opposite side that'd begun to go around a middle-aged woman who was afraid to get on the escalator.

Later that evening, after I'd finished sharing that story with my mother, my mother said: *Isn't it amazing how we sometimes allow fear to stop us from getting where we need to go?*

2)
I'm thankful for being given a mother who continues to teach me how much of an act of faith, and how beautiful a prayer, being courageous is.

3)
Just this morning, while she stood in front of a sink full of soapy water, washing the refrigerator shelves, I sat at the kitchen table and listened to her muse about how she couldn't get an early morning appointment for her next chemo treatment beause of the people who have to be there for five and six hours.

I'm thankful for the light, she said. *Taking our blessings and running with them is the best way to fight this battle.*

Alex: 2

I was driving home
from work today
listening to a news story
on the radio
where a woman
told the reporter
how she also
had to come out of the closet
so she could
openly support
her gay son.
Once, while in Pattaya,
I went to a nightclub
in Boyztown
where, following
the swim show,
a pageant
of beautiful bodies
peacocked
around the auction block
each with a number tag
clipped to his hip
by the waist band
of white bikini briefs
in hopes of being bought
by a boyfriend for the night
before their song ended
and the next crop
of courtesans
took the stage.

Ten months later, back in Bangkok,
Alex and I
were laying together in bed
when he said:
Well, If you
and your mom
are so close,
why haven't you
already told her
you're not
'romatically interested'
in women?

The Hospital: 1

A Prayer:

I was walking
through the foyer
on my way
to the cafeteria
contemplating
an interview
I'd heard
earlier this morning
on NPR
–with a guy
who said
he joined the army
to know
what it felt like
to kill
another
human being–
when I saw a woman
sitting on a bench
holding an infant
with a feeding tube
that started
at the bottom
of a drip bag
hanging
from a portable IV stand,
and was taped
to his left cheek

before being threaded up
into his left nostril,
then down his throat
and into his stomach.
There's a small sign
upstairs
in our breakroom
on the table
next to the computer
that says:
Welcome to life,
it's precious.

Amen.

Neupogen

Please don't touch the bed
My bones hurt

Like nerves
Like needles

I took my medicine too late
I won't wait so long next time

This is an awakening
Spasms equal pain

I'm glad I got so much done earlier

This is bad now
But it will get better soon

This is war
Thank God we're not chasing a tumor

I'm learning a different way of living
And am gaining a new appreciation
    for feeling good

Would you mind taking some notes for me
There should be a notepad on the sewing table
    and a multi-color pen on the night stand

Ready? Okay:

8:00 am– *32 oz of water*
2:00 pm– *Sunchips with a burrito*
      – *Sore throat: talked to nurse, no fever*
2:50 pm– *2 Vicadin*
2:30 pm– *1 cup of tea*

Thank you

I need to make sure
my body has what it needs
to carry me as long as it can

History

I hooked-up
with a guy
in hopes
of a good quickie,
but I was unable
to make
our situation work.
So instead,
I suggested we
put our clothes back on
and have a conversation.
He told me
he was a bank manager
with a degree
in grapic design;
and that he'd never
seen the ocean,
but wanted
to go to Italy because
he'd fallen in love
with Renaissance art
while studying
in university–
which he attended
in small town Montana.
While there, he drove
long miles to meet men
who didn't look anything like
their profile pictures,
but with whom

he fooled around with anyway
because there were no gays
where he was at.
He said he was lonely,
and wanted to find a way
to meet other guys
that didn't include gay bars
and wasn't superglued to "just sex,"
but that he didn't know
where else to go.
He told me that Denver
is the furthest he's been away from home,
"Which is why I'm here,"
he said. *"So that I can be who I am."*

2)
And maybe finding yourself isn't as hard as accepting what you've found and making something beautiful out of it.

And maybe love is allowing each person you cross paths with to open your heart a little more.

Hair: 1

I didn't wear
Eye make-up today

I figured when I
Start chemo

I'll lose my brows
And lashes too

The lady yesterday
Said the doctors

Told her she'd lose
All her hair

They didn't tell her
She'd lose it all at once

She said
It was traumatic

So I figured I should
Start preparing myself

Mom, What is God Teaching You: 1

I used to be afraid
of being a single mom.

I think that's what
kept me married,

because we were poor
and the car

was always breaking down
and I didn't know

how to fix a car
but your dad did.

But, God kept showing me
it'd all be okay.

Prayer is important.
you have to have faith,

because that's what
gives you the courage to walk

even though sometimes
you don't always know

where your're going.
You have to walk,

because if you don't
you'll get stuck

under the mountain
and fear will drown you.

Sometimes just standing
is walking.

But you have to get up
and stand.

I think if I would have stayed married
I would have wilted.

My Mom and God

I told God again
I don't understand
the reason
for all these close calls.

God said: sit down
and I'll tell you.

Penpals: 11

This morning I heard a comedian on the radio explain how life is hard because it's a job and we all get paid $13.50 per hour.

And how, when the soul leaves the body God pays you and then begins going over your sins and charges you for each one.

And how, if you can't afford to pay then, you have to be reborn and earn enough money to pay off your debt.

As I listened I was reminded of the only Dharma Talk I ever attended in Thailand. The monk ended his sermon by saying: *There are no victims, only karma.*

—

I lost both of my grandfathers to brain cancer, and my uncle to lung cancer. And now there are a lot of women in my camp fighting this awful, malignant demon: my mom, a friend from church. The sister of another friend's daughter-in-law died in May when a tumor returned and set up shop in the lining around the precious jewel on the left side of her chest. There was nothing the doctors could do.

Anyway, this morning, after showering, I stepped out of the tub, looked at myself in the mirror and remembered the Zen story about a guy who climbed over the edge of a cliff to escape a tiger that was chasing him. But when he looks down he sees another tiger. Then he notices a little mouse nibbling at the vine he's holding on to for dear life. He also sees a lovely bunch of berries growing out of a patch of grass. He looks up, he looks down, he looks at the mouse, then he picks the berries and enjoys each one–like a short vacation before returning to work.

I'm thankful for that story. I'm learning that finding something to be thankful for keeps me happy. But, it's a difficult practice—like forgiving, or remembering to take my vitamins everyday.

—

I'm not sure why I wrote this note and sent it to you. But, I do know that at the beginning of this piece of paper I was afraid, and now I'm not. So thanks for that.

The Sunrise

Do you remember how I fired the first doctor
who was gonna take out my ovaries?

That was because three weeks before surgery
I dreamed I'd died on the operation table.

I saw her coming out to talk
with you all in the waiting room.

I woke up hearing you all telling
that story for the rest of your lives.

So I told her: *Sorry, I'm not
going under with you.*

It's strange how I process things,
you know? And now, since I start

chemo next week, everyone at work
wants to take me out to lunch.

But, I can't go. All they want to know
is how I'm doing.

I'm so angry at the whole situation
that everytime I talk about it, I cry.

Anyway, did you see how the sunrise
made everything purple this morning?

A House

It's so funny
how different

a house looks
from the driveway

than it does
from the hallway.

I look in the mirror
and can't believe

this fight for my life
is going on inside of me,

I try hard
to stay healthy:

I eat right.
I do yoga every morning.

I go to the gym.
I'm learning to rest.

I sometimes wonder
why my body is so unhappy.

What did I do
to make it

not like me
soooo much?

It just goes to show
you can't judge

a book
by its cover.

A Dove

Yesterday morning,
while walking my dog
in the big field
across the street from our home,
I saw a Peaceful Dove
laid out on its back
with spread wings and
feet curled-up to its belly,
looking as though its body
had frozen, mid-flight,
and fallen from the sky.
Last night, before sleep,
I laid in bed imagining
walking through the garden section
of the hardware store
and happening upon
a small plastic blue pot
holding a beautiful flower
whose leafless green stem
was wigged in a bouquet
of white whorled florets
with golden teabowl hearts.
Then came the memory of the day
my Great Grandma Della died
and how the mortician and his assistant
gently lifted her little body
from the hospital bed
and placed it inside a black body bag
that they carefully zipped
from foot-to-collarbone;

—we'd requested
they not cover her face.
The two men then slowly rolled her out
to a black minivan
on a wobbly stretcher.

Bowling

This morning
my mom
was awakened
by a crippling pain
in her left arm
that was triggered
by the sleeve
she has to wear
to control
the lymphedema.
All this is like a ball
coming down
the bowling alley
trying to knock me down,
she said, *It gets*
discouraging sometimes.
But I'm not giving in.
I just think
I'm a little nervous
about starting
radiation. But,
I'm a child of the King
and He gave me tools.
And I use them.

Penpals: 12

Last night, I told Lenny about the stable boy I knew in Thailand who was fired from his job with the horses and sent to live with his uncle in a worker's camp of skyscraper builders in Bangkok for trying to protect his older sister from a glue-sniffing groom with red teeth; and how the boy was the second of four children, none of whom had ever had a birthday party because their parents, Nam and Jo, couldn't remember when any of them were born.

There's a Khmer proverb that says: *The rice field is their university. The hoe, their pen.* It reminds me of the day I asked the reason Nam and Jo's kids weren't in school, and was told that if we didn't keep the servants dumb, they'd kill us.

When the evening with Lenny ended, I went home, got in bed and–since I don't know how I'm feeling until I ask myself to find words–wrote in my journal. Then sleep came, and with it, the high school memory of how I used to wonder whether suicide would be more beneficial than growing into a future I'm afraid of and calling it life.

—

This morning, I was on my yoga mat–in lotus pose, following the breath–when I heard my heart say: *you know you don't have to fold your legs into a figure-eight to find peace, it's not that difficult. You just have to stop affording yourself the luxury of making contemporary decisions with historical pain. You're gonna twist your body into a pretzel and someone's gonna have to come and shake you loose.*

Hair: 6

1)

My hair started coming out in handfuls. So, we got the clippers and Anna cut it off.

I did my backbends this morning,–not as deep as I wanted go. But, it's time to get back in the gym. My body is like 'let's go sweat.'

Come here. See the spots where the hair has completely run away?

I have to go get my head shaved. I'm afraid I'll get razor bumps if I shave it myself.

Choosing to live is a conscious choice:

I'm not just gonna let some thing or some one come in and kick my ass–not without a fight.

2)

I was talking to Anna, telling her how it was thinning.

She said I needed to just cut it off, or else I'd wake up one morning with my braids on my pillow and I'd be pissed because it would make me late to work.

3)

I hope my going through this, and you all walking through it with me, gives each of you something you can hold on to:

We all have our challenges. But, everything is only one thing.

We can only walk as far as our legs can stretch: one step at a time.

Mom, What's God Teaching You: 2

I think
I've figured out

why this cancer
comeback came:

I used to only want to live
long enough

to see my kids grow up.
I didn't see myself

retireing or getting old,
I only saw up to

where I'm at now.
It's like when you

told me about the time
you read through

the journal you had
when you were eighteen,

and realized
that the prayers

you prayed
ten years ago

were just now
being answered.

This Evening

1)

We'd met at Café Max, on Colfax between Columbine and Josephine–right across the street from Sun Mart. He was wearing blue jeans and a t-shirt with a picture of a squirrel holding a martini with an acorn where an olive should be. When I saw him walk in I smiled and invited him to join me. We ordered a loose-leaf blend that smelled like camp fire.

During the course of our conversation, he shared how, just this afternoon, in his art therapy group, he asked the kids to each create an abstract representation of their time in treatment so far. And how one girl drew a picture of a hunter and a person and a deer on a piece of black construction paper. She explains: *The hunter is drugs, and alcohol, and suicide. The deer is me. The little pink person is all the people trying to save the deer–staff, my parents. And the little pink person saves the deer from the hunter and the hunter goes away. And the deer grows and goes on to become strong.*

2)

Two hours later, he was sprawled out on my bed like a cross street. The feeling of his dick in my mouth reminded me of peeled Rambutan fruit. His phone rang. He opened his eyes, answered, then hung up and said it was his brother and that they were waiting for him to get home so that they could cut the birthday cake. He sighed then asked if we should hurry-up and come. *No,* I said, *No need to rush.* We kissed, got dressed, kissed again, then I walked him downstairs and saw him out.

I spent the rest of the evening at my desk trying to construct a poem around the image in my mind of an old woman sitting in a rocking chair. Her hands are resting on her belly, just above the neatly folded bend of a beautifully stitched appliqué quilt. The quilt has a blue and white floral print sky behind a little light-weight, virgin-white cotton country house with a brown roof and matching shutters edging four window panes hemmed on with strands of indigo floss silk.

Walking: 1

The wind carried the laughter
of invisible children
playing in the neighborhood
next door to the field
where my dog galloped around in circles
like she was herding sheep
while I walked along
singing a prayer and wondering
what little furry buds bursting open
on the branch of a pussy willow
would sound like
before I stopped to watch
a baby garter snake
slither across the dirt path
it had a gray and tan
checkerboard pattern
between the white stripes
down the sides of its body
the two tips of its tongue were dark
like a fountain pen point
dipped in black or blue liquid ink
I spent the rest of our walk
listening to my footsteps

Hair: 2

I'm sitting here
with my bald head
trying to see
how I can feel beautiful

The Hospital: 2

I was walking
from the cafeteria
when I passed
a little boy
sitting in a wheelchair
with a black seat belt
fastened snugly
across his lap.
His was wearing
a metal halo
held in place by pins
protruding from his skull
like a crown of thorns.
A soldered on rod
arced over top his cranium
–from ear-to-ear–
like a rainbow
from which a white
spine straightening string
was pulled tight
like a person between
the upward call
and a downward craving.
He is over here
and healing is over there.
Between them:
a mountain with snow-capped peak
in summer.
His dad was pushing him
across the lobby

toward the small choir of carolers
who'd come to sing
Christmas songs
for the children.

Church Folk

This evening, we were at a party, and this preacher's wife asked my mom if she was a member of a church. My mom said: I used to go to church all the time—my sons were ushers; me and my daughter sang in the choir—but, when my grandma passed I didn't want to go anymore. I figured God wasn't gonna be mad at me for focusing on my family instead of struggling, as a single parent, to raise my kids as members of a community of people who only act like they love each other on Sundays.

That's also when I decided I wasn't gonna get re-married while my kids were still young, because I didn't want to put them through the possiblity of another divorce.

I used to tell them they wouldn't be able to look back and wonder why I was their friend and not their mother. That's what kept me going when we were poor and I was working like a slave:

I wanted them to know they where important.

People used to tell me, *You can't put everything into your kids.* But, in my way of thinking, if you don't put everything into your kids, why have them?

Hallelujah

I've heard it said that for our spirit to come and experiance time, we are born of a woman who carries us in arms we created;–that our path to heaven is found in her footsteps.

This morning she shared what happened yesterday at the radiologist's office; and how she made the doctor so angry with questions about her treatment, that he told her she wasn't special. *Maybe I'm not special to you,* she said, *because you're the doctor and this is your job. But I'm special to me and everyone I love who loves me back, so is every one of your other patients, which is why we're all here: to get help saving what's left of the rest of our lives. Now,* she said, *please answer my questions.*

And he did, she said. *Our lives are only carefree until reality sets in, At the beginning of all this, they told me everything was okay. But, in the back of my mind I told myself not to get so tired that you trust these doctors with your life, because if you do and they're wrong (and they were) then you're dead.*
—
These side effects of radiation are a beast. But it was either live or die. And if this is the price I have to pay to have peace in my heart and know I've done everything I can to keep the cancer away if it comes back, then okay.

Lately, though, I've had a hard time seeing the light, and so have been going to the store every morning before my appontment and buying myself a yellow rose so I can take the sunshine in with me.

She said, *Yesterday I felt so bad because my skin is starting to peel and I had a headache and I was trying to leave when the sump-pump alarm went off and I was just ready to throw my hands up. But I stopped myself and said ,'You got this, slow down, take a deep breath, because I really believe–that on the other side of this–the sky is blue.'. In reality my situation is like a fudge brownie served with sprinkle covered vanilla ice cream compared to most people at the radiation clinic. There's a woman there who'd been in remission from breast cancer for fifteen years and they found a tumor on her lung. Today she was there with her daughter and grandaughter.*

We're not chasing a tumor. I'm thankful for that. Thank God for that. Hallelujah!

A Poem

On the bus to Thailand I was seated next to a young, Cambodian monk named Shray who said he was on his way to meet a French man he'd met on the internet. Then he began sharing his plan of going to university to study tourism and his dreams of world travel; and later, wondered if I starved myself: *Since you're so skinny*, he said, as he wrapped his fingers around my bicep and gently squeezed.

I spent the rest of the ride reading a book in a re-assigned seat next to an old woman dressed in sandals, dark pants and a purple polo shirt with pink trim around the collar and sleeves. The book was by a prostitute whose career began the night her mom sold her virginity to a tourist for eight hundred dollars. She wrote about what it was like to stare at her naked, flat-chested reflection in the hotel room mirror while blood flowed down from between her thighs like streams of cherry colored tears.

—

My first day in Bangkok began when I woke-up, walked over to the window and looked down to the street, at a scantily clad Siamese woman in stilettos arguing with a drunk, young foreigner who kept asking if they'd fucked. *"No,"* she said, *"but I suck you."* A few minutes later, the man stood up from the edge of the chair he was sitting in and knocked the wind out of the woman with a knee to the gut.

—

I've learned that sometimes, all I can do is go to my room lock the door and cry my eyes out on my pillow when I'd rather be helping to heal someone else's hurting heart; and that heartache is the womb of wisdom giving birth to the grasp of things as they are because that's how they're supposed to be; and that suffering is darkness with light inside the time on earth for those of us who are rediscovering our native loveliness, which is what life is.

And what is money if nothing more than the ability to not have to bow your head to whomever you can afford not to respect if you don't want to?

—

Before the matter was resolved between the trick and his treat, my phone began to ring. So, I walked over to the nightstand to see who was calling. It was my mommy.

I spent the rest of that day at Jatujack Market, where, when I walked to the end of the pet section, I saw a small group of hysterically excited men and boys gathered around in a circle that they either cheered or groaned into each time one of the scrappy roosters drew blood from his brother with claws that'd been filed into razor-edged daggers.

As the two fighting birds grew more exhausted it soon became clear which of them was going to die.

—

When evening came, I passed a beggar missing both his legs below the knee. He was laying face down in the middle of the sidewalk with an empty plastic cup held out in front of his head.

Rainbow Alley

He reminded me
so much of myself

when I was younger
as he explained

how kids bully him
at school because

his favorite T.V. show
is 'My Little Pony'

But, the reason
I'm here, he said,

is because my dad
punched me in the face

and called me
awful names

when he found out
I have a boyfriend

When I asked
what he'd like to work on today

He said, *Brainstorming*
things I'd like

to talk to
my family about

Tattoos

I'm tired of my arm.
I have to deal with

this Lymphadema everyday.
But, at least I'm not

preparing to die;
or picking out a burial plot;

or what I want to wear
at my funeral;

or what color casket I want.
But, I decided

if cancer was gonna kill me
I wasn't gonna wear a wig.

I was gonna go down bald
with a tattoo-head.

At the memorial service
people would be like

"What did Lori's kids do?"
And ya'll'd be like "Nothin'

–this is just her way of saying
'Fuck the world.' "

But, I'm grateful
I'm not chasing a tumor.

This Morning

"I am leaving you. God bless you. This country and this world are not for me."
—Isa Sahmarli

This morning
I spent an hour
before work
searching
for an honest prayer to pray.
But, the only thing that came
was the memory
of a giggly little boy
I passed
on my way home
from dinner
one evening.
He was running around
in crazy zigzags lines
in street lamp glow
chasing his granddad's shadow
on the sidewalk.
That little boy was so happy,
he made me happy, too.
But this is an ugly world
we live in. Things
don't always turn out
the way we'd like them to.
We grow up as children
thinking everything
is going to be
wonderful in our lives;

and we're going to have
wonderful jobs
and wonderful families
and wonderful opportunities,
then reality sets in
and it's not
what we want it to be.
And the only thing
that comes clear
in a world that isn't
is that people are people
and not everyone
can handle life.

Jesus Christ Loves You

Earlier today I heard on the radio about Arizona's governer vetoing a bill that would allow refusal of service to anyone who disagreed with a business owner's religion and couldn't help but wonder how for all of our intense efforts to do things like we've always done them, when will we have the courage to admit it's not working anymore. I remember being in college and thinking how maybe converting to Catholicism or the Orthodox Church and becoming a monk would temper the expectation of my being attracted to women out of fear that my attraction to men was an emissary of the devil trying to steal my soul.

At that time I was volunteering as a youth mentor in an evangelical ministry for teens called *The Well*. One night, after the service ended, I walked through the lobby and on the way out to my car, passed the pastor, a bald, wide backed man, who was wearing blue jeans and a yellow t-shirt that had *Jesus Christ Loves You* plastered on the back like a four-color, big glossy billboard on the side of the highway promising product for inventory no one has.
—

Fast-forward five years, a few months, and some days, and I'm in Thailand on a hot afternoon, and I'm out to lunch with the family I train horses for and one of their friends who's defending her hypothesis about Global Warming making all the good men gay with the fact that she's having trouble finding a suitable husband for her daughter,–a student in her last year of medical school. That same night I was rolling around in the sheets with a guy from the gym whose cock was a masterpiece. After he got dressed and prepared to leave I gave him my number then closed the door behind him hoping he'd call so we could meet up again,–maybe for dinner, or tea, or a walk in the park.

The next morning I woke up and did what I always did every morning before work: I thanked God for the day, then swept the floor of my flat with a little traditional Thai broom whose bristles were made from the reedy acrobatic hairstrands of dried rice straw hays that had been tied together and woven around one end of a short bamboo stick,–which archs the spine forward into a hump when you stretch your arm out then pull dust toward you in gentle dragging motions.

Salvation

This evening
there was a story
on the radio
in which
a teenaged mother
wrote
a thank you letter
to her school
for saving her
from sinking
into drugs
and gangs
and guns
like old food
going down
the drain.
She said,
I could feel
the spikes
on my toes.
She said
I was sinking
like other people
I've known
who've
given up.
She said,
Once my poetry teacher
told us
to be guided

by our love
when we don't know
what else to do.
So, she said,
I'm raising my son
and studying.

The End

Today was my mom's
last of thirty-five

radiation treatments
which were proceeded

by four rounds
of chemo and a surgery.

This morning after she returned home
from the radiologist's office

we went to the Pancake House
for breakfast.

While we waited for our food
my mom explained

how good it felt
to be walking on top of waters

that would have drown her
had she stayed on a sinking boat.

*Look at how far
we've come by faith,* she said.

Which is the miracle isn't it:
to be able to stop

and look back
at what you've survived

and then
keep going.